absolutely avocado

Rio Nuevo Publishers®
P.O. Box 5250, Tucson, Arizona 85703-0250
(520) 623-9558, www.rionuevo.com

Text and photography © 2006 by Rio Nuevo Publishers. Food styling by
Tracy Vega. Many thanks to AJ's Fine Foods and to Jeannine Brookshire for
providing beautiful settings and amenities for the photo shoots for this book.

Photography credits as follows:
W. Ross Humphreys: pages 2-3, 60, 72, front cover
Robin Stancliff: pages 4 (left), 5, 20, 33, 38, 41, 53, 65, 75, 79
Katy Parks Wilson: pages 4 (right), 10, 22, back cover

Library of Congress Cataloging-in-Publication Data
Duncann, Geraldine.
Absolutely avocado / Geraldine Duncann.
    p. cm. -- (Cook west series)
Includes index.
ISBN-13: 978-1-887896-89-4 (pbk.)
ISBN-10: 1-887896-89-9 (pbk.)
1. Cookery (Avocado) 2. Cookery, American--Southwestern
style. I. Title. II. Series.
TX813.A9D86 2006
641.6'4653--dc22

                            2006001073

Design: Karen Schober, Seattle, Washington.

Printed in Korea.
10 9 8 7 6 5 4 3 2

absolutely
avocado

GERALDINE DUNCANN

COOK WEST
SERIES

contents

xxxxxx

There's more to avocados than green goo to scoop up with a tortilla chip. When I was growing up in California, my family had a never-ending supply of avocados at a ridiculously inexpensive price, so Mama put them in everything she could think of. She diced them into her cornbread batter and added them to waffles. Along with the avocado, she would lay two pieces of bacon on top of the batter before closing the lid. The end result was a beautiful toasty waffle with crispy bacon on top, bits of creamy avocado throughout, and the whole thing bespeaking a light essence of the bacon's smokiness. Although my mother put avocados in virtually everything, I can't ever remember her making guacamole. That didn't come into our recipe repertoire until sometime in the 1950s, when dips of all sorts first exploded onto the American entertainment scene.

The Codawada Lady (*codawada* was as close to pronouncing "avocado" as I could come as a kid) lived at the far end of the lake, where she and her husband maintained a large avocado grove—one of the first commercial groves in California. Every other Wednesday, she drove around the lake in her big Woody station wagon, selling her wares. Overripe, squishy ones she gave us by the bucketful to feed to our turkeys. A flat of 24 huge, perfect avocados cost 50 cents. When she informed my dad that the price had gone up to sixty cents a flat, he gasped in horror.

It was because of this inexhaustible supply of beautiful avocados that my mother took to experimenting with them. One of our family's favorite recipes was a salad made of citrus fruits and avocados. We had orange, lemon, grapefruit, kumquat, and tangerine trees on our property, so there was some form of citrus in season all year long. Some of our avocado experiments were less than rewarding. I think it's best, for example, that Mama's recipe for chicken with rice and avocado stuffing went to the grave with her. However, her deep-fried crab and avocado puffs were spectacular, as were the avocado and chicken salad sandwiches.

Through the years I have continued my mother's avocado research and experimentation, sometimes with huge success and sometimes not. The end result is that the recipes you find here are guaranteed to take your avocado enjoyment far beyond guacamole, and will allow you to use these wonderful, nutritious fruits in a wealth of delicious ways.

A BIT OF AVOCADO HISTORY

It is believed that avocados existed in Mexico as early as 7,000 B.C. and that a variety was cultivated as early as 750 B.C. Archaeologists have found seeds buried with Incan mummies in Peru dating from 500 B.C. Thus horticulturalists identify avocados—along with corn, figs, tobacco, and sugarcane—as "cultigens," or cultivated species that have been domesticated for so many centuries and have gone through such drastic transformations that their true ancestry is now unknown. All that is certain is that the avocado probably originated in south-central Mexico.

The Aztec name for the fruit was *aoacatl* or *ahuacatl*. The word for tree was *quahuitl*. Thus the avocado tree became the *ahuacaquahuitl*. The conquistadores had difficulty with the Aztec language, so aoacatl soon became *auacate*. An English merchant traveling in the 1580s called it the "Alvacata" in an English publication, and in 1696, naturalist Sir Hans Sloane wrote about "the Avocado."

In California, the first reference to avocados appears in 1856 when a tree was imported, along with other fruit trees, by Dr. Thomas J. White, who lived near Los Angeles. In the early 1890s, Juan Murrieta, also of Los Angeles, imported quite a few seeds from Mexico. This stimulated interest in the commercial possibilities, and by the early 1900s numerous experimental plantings were underway.

There are over 500 varieties of avocado, only a few of which are grown commercially, and the Hass is by far the most popular, representing over 80 percent of the commercial crop. Like California's Zinfandel wine grape, the Hass was a rather mysterious accidental hybrid, acquired in the late 1920s by a postman named Hass. He soon realized the superior quality of the fruits borne on this lone tree and began cultivating it. All

Hass avocados are descendants of that same tree, which finally died from a fungus in 2002.

California currently produces 95 percent of the United States commercial crop, most of which is grown from San Diego north to San Luis Obispo, with the largest concentration of commercial groves now in the Carpinteria Valley.

SELECTING AVOCADOS

Avocados, like tomatoes, are picked green for shipping and continue to ripen after being picked. Unlike tomatoes, however, avocados picked green and allowed to ripen off the tree do not have diminished flavor. Avocados can go from stone-hard to very soft and ripe in just a few days. If you do not intend to use it for several days, purchasing a hard avocado is fine. Bring it home, put it in a brown paper bag, and leave it at room temperature. Also placing an apple or a banana in the bag will accelerate the process, as these fruits give off ethylene gas, a ripening agent. Once ripened, avocados may be stored in the refrigerator for a day or two. If you plan on using your avocados on the same day you purchase them, select ones that give a little when you gently press them with your thumb.

NUTRITION

Avocados are an excellent and healthy source of nutrition. They are quite caloric, containing a good bit of fat, but it is all good fat. Your waistline, if you over-indulge, may not appreciate them, but your heart certainly will. Avocados contain 60 percent more potassium than bananas. They are also a great source of antioxidants, and their low sugar and starch content makes them an ideal food for diabetics or hypoglycemics— eating small slices throughout the day can help keep sugar in balance. Mashed avocado also makes a perfect baby food, especially with other mashed fresh fruit.

Guacamole Plain and Simple

xxxxxx

Some folks believe that placing the seed of the avocado in your bowl of guacamole will prevent it from turning brown. I have never found this to be true. Sometimes guacamole turns brown and sometimes it doesn't. I think it depends on how much lime juice is used.

Combine avocado, garlic, onion, crushed chile, and lime juice, mixing well. Season to taste with salt and pepper.

Makes about 2 cups, depending on size of avocados

4 ripe avocados, mashed

1 clove garlic, very finely minced

$1/4$ cup finely chopped onion

Pinch of crushed chile pepper, or to taste

Juice of 1 fresh lime

Salt and freshly ground black pepper

Guacamole with an Attitude

XXXXXX

Makes about 3 cups, depending on size of avocados

4 ripe avocados, mashed

1 large tomato, seeded and finely chopped

1/2 cup finely chopped sweet purple onion

4–5 cloves garlic, very finely minced

1 green onion, chopped fine, including the green top

1/2 cup finely chopped celery

1 fresh jalapeño chile pepper, seeded and finely chopped, or to taste

1/4 cup finely chopped fresh cilantro, or to taste (reserve 1 sprig for garnish)

1 teaspoon taco seasoning

Juice of 1–2 fresh limes (reserve 1 slice for garnish)

Salt and freshly ground black pepper

This is excellent as a dip with chips or cut fresh vegetables. Try it as a sandwich spread. Put a dollop on a leaf of crisp lettuce, add a few slices of tomato, and serve it as a salad, or use it as an accompaniment to foods such as burritos and soft tacos.

Mix all ingredients together. Garnish with a slice of lime and a sprig of fresh cilantro.

Avocado Crab Puffs

xxxxxx

These delectable fritters have long been a family favorite. Served with ranch dressing for dipping, they make an excellent light lunch or great party snacks. For variations, you can add a few drops of sesame oil or ½ teaspoon of grated fresh ginger-root. Or substitute Chinese five-spice powder for the nutmeg, sesame seed for the Parmesan, teriyaki sauce for the ranch dressing, and/or cilantro for the parsley garnish.

Pour about 4 inches of vegetable oil in a heavy pot or deep fryer and heat to about 360 degrees F.

Meanwhile, place the butter and olive oil in a heavy skillet and gently sauté the onion and garlic until translucent. Add Sherry to de-glaze the pan, and continue to sauté for another minute or so. Remove to a large bowl. Add the avocado and mash thoroughly.

Add the crabmeat, Cheddar, Swiss cheese, olives, roasted pepper, parsley, lemon zest, lemon juice, nutmeg, cayenne, and egg, and mix well. Season to taste with salt and pepper and add enough flour to form a firm batter. To test for proper temperature, drop a spoonful of batter into the hot oil. Fry for 2–3 minutes, or until golden brown, then break it in half to test for doneness. Since there is so little flour, these will not have the rather cakey texture of many fritters. The inside will be soft and creamy from the avocado and cheeses.

Once the oil is the correct temperature, use 2 teaspoons to form dollops of batter about the size of large walnuts. Fry only

Makes about 2 dozen

Vegetable oil for deep frying

1 tablespoon butter

1 tablespoon olive oil

$1/2$ medium-size onion, chopped fine

3–4 cloves garlic, finely minced

2 tablespoons cream Sherry

1 large avocado, pitted and peeled

1 $1/2$ cups flaked crabmeat

$1/2$ cup grated extra-sharp white Cheddar

$1/2$ cup grated Swiss cheese (such as Emmentaler or Gruyère)

$1/4$ cup chopped black olives

$1/4$ cup finely chopped roasted red bell pepper (directions follow)

$1/4$ cup finely chopped fresh parsley

1 teaspoon lemon zest

1 teaspoon lemon juice

$1/2$ teaspoon ground nutmeg

Pinch of cayenne pepper

1 large egg, beaten

Salt and freshly ground black pepper

About $1/2$ cup all-purpose flour

(ingredients continue on next page)

6–8 at a time. When golden brown, remove from the oil with a slotted spoon and drain on paper towels.

Grated Parmesan cheese

Fresh parsley, for garnish

Lemon or lime wedges, for garnish

To serve, dust with Parmesan cheese and serve with your favorite ranch dressing for dipping. Garnish the plate with fresh parsley and wedges of lemon or lime.

ROASTING BELL PEPPERS AND CHILES

To roast chiles and peppers, choose ones with as few convolutions to their surface as possible. If you have a gas stove, hold each pepper over the flame with a pair of tongs, turning to roast evenly. Roast until the skins are mostly blackened and blistered, then put the pepper in a brown paper bag or wrap it in cloth or an old tea towel. Let it steam 3–4 minutes, then rinse under cold running water, rubbing off the blackened skin. Next, remove the stem and seeds, rinse well, and set aside to drain. Do not roast more peppers at a time than you can finish cleaning before they become completely cold. Otherwise it will be difficult to get the charred skin off. And yes, you can use an electric stove! Simply lay your peppers directly on the element, turning frequently with tongs (not a fork) until they are blackened and blistered.

Grilled Avocado Shish Kebabs

XXXXXX

A favorite for outdoor grilling.

Makes 1 dozen

Peel and devein the prawns, leaving the tails intact. Set aside.

Cut the avocados into bite-size chunks and sprinkle with lime juice to prevent them from turning brown.

To assemble, put the prawns, pineapple chunks, and avocado onto skewers, alternating, using about 3 prawns per skewer. Wrap the strips of bacon around the other ingredients, barber-pole fashion. Secure it on the skewer at both ends. Sprinkle with salt and pepper to taste.

To make the basting sauce, combine the soy sauce, vinegar, olive oil, sugar, gingerroot, and sesame oil; mix well, and use this to baste the shish kebabs as they are grilling.

Place them on the grill or under the broiler and cook to desired degree of doneness, turning once or twice. Baste with the sauce during cooking. Be gentle or the delicate avocado will fall off the skewers.

36 raw prawns

2–3 large ripe but firm avocados

Juice of 2–3 fresh limes

Fresh or canned pineapple chunks

12 thin slices of bacon

Salt and freshly ground black pepper

$1/2$ cup soy sauce

2 tablespoons rice vinegar

2 tablespoons olive oil

2 tablespoons sugar

1 teaspoon grated fresh gingerroot

1–2 drops sesame oil

Avocado Stuffed Eggs

xxxxx

Makes 2 dozen

12 hard-boiled eggs

1 large avocado, diced very small

Juice of 1 lime

2 cloves roasted garlic (directions follow), minced

2 tablespoons chopped black olives

1/4 cup finely crumbled feta cheese

2 tablespoons finely minced sweet purple onion

1 tablespoon finely minced fresh chives

Minced fresh cilantro, for garnish

Ranch dressing

Salt and freshly ground black pepper

The amount of ranch dressing to use is a matter of taste. Some people like their stuffed eggs rather on the dry side, while others like them quite moist. It's your call!

Peel, rinse, and dry the eggs. Cut them in half lengthwise. Remove the yolks and set the whites aside. Using the back of a spoon, force the egg yolks through a sieve and into a bowl.

Dice the avocado and squeeze a bit of the lime juice over it to prevent browning. Add the avocado to the sieved yolks, then add the garlic, olives, feta, onion, chives, and cilantro.

Add as much ranch dressing as needed to stir into an appropriate consistency to stuff into the eggs. Season to taste with salt and pepper and toss gently, being careful not to "mash" the ingredients. Stuff the egg whites, arrange on a plate, and garnish with sprigs of fresh cilantro. Spread any leftover filling on toast points, or use as a sandwich spread.

ROASTING GARLIC

Wipe a nonstick skillet lightly with olive oil, then pour in as many peeled, whole cloves of garlic as you wish, but making sure you have them only one layer deep. Turn the heat to medium-low and allow the garlic to just barely become golden on the bottom, then stir. Continue until all cloves are golden brown on all sides and soft when pressed, about 30 minutes. Once done, allow them to cool, and store in a covered jar in the refrigerator.

Avocado Tapenade

xxxxxx

This makes a wonderful appetizer or snack. Though many dishes are called "tapenade," if it doesn't have capers in it, it isn't a true tapenade, because tapenade comes from tapeno, *the French Provençal word for caper.*

Preheat the oven to broil.

Place the garlic, olives, capers, anchovies, onion, and olive oil into the workbowl of a blender or food processor and pulse until chopped but not puréed. If the mixture seems too thick, add 1–2 tablespoons more olive oil. Remove to a bowl and add the avocado, stirring gently so as not to mash it. Season to taste with salt and pepper. Spread on toasted slices of baguette, sprinkle lightly with Parmesan cheese, and pop under the broiler for 2–3 minutes.

Makes about 2 cups

2 cloves garlic, chopped

1 can (4$1/4$ ounces) chopped black olives, drained

3 tablespoons capers, drained

2 anchovy fillets, chopped

$1/4$ cup chopped sweet purple onion

$1/4$ cup olive oil

1 large avocado, diced small

Salt and freshly ground black pepper

Sliced baguette loaf

Parmesan cheese

Smoked Salmon-Wrapped Avocado

xxxxxx

For a delectable and incredibly simple appetizer, try this California variation on the old melon-and-prosciutto theme.

Cut each avocado half into 4 lengthwise slices and sprinkle with lime juice to prevent browning. Wrap each avocado slice in a thin slice of smoked salmon and secure with a toothpick. Add a grinding of pepper over each and serve chilled.

Makes 16

2 ripe yet firm avocados, halved

Juice of 1 lime

16 thin slices smoked salmon (about 4 ounces)

Freshly ground black pepper

Avocado Baked Brie with Cranberry Chutney

xxxxxx

Serves about 6

1 small round of brie

1/2 cup mashed avocado

1/2 cup cranberry chutney

1 sheet packaged, frozen puff pastry, thawed

Egg wash (1 egg beaten with 1 tablespoon cold water)

This twist on baked brie provides a truly delicious and quite unusual starter. If you can't find cranberry chutney, you can mix together 6 tablespoons of other prepared chutney with 2 tablespoons of canned whole cranberries.

Preheat the oven to 350 degrees F.

Spread the top of the round of brie with avocado, followed by the chutney. Lay a sheet of puff pastry over the top and carefully flip the cheese and pastry over so that the pastry is on the bottom. Trim the pastry so that it will be just large enough to securely wrap around and encase the brie.

Baste the edges of the pastry with egg wash and pinch the edges together to seal. Place the brie, sealed side down, on a parchment-lined baking sheet. Using a small sharp knife, make several small slashes in the pastry to allow steam to escape during baking. Baste once more with egg wash.

If you wish, you may cut the pastry scraps into decorative leaves or flowers to decorate the top of the pastry. Place in the center of the oven and bake until the pastry is a beautiful golden brown, about 30 minutes. Serve warm with crackers or toasted baguette slices.

Avocado Party Triangles

xxxxxx

Creamy avocado and melted cheese combine with flaky pastry for an elegant hors d'ouevre. Try adding baby shrimp, crab-meat, minced grilled chicken, or minced ham. I particularly love them with the addition of smoked oysters.

Preheat oven to 350 degrees F.

Heat the olive oil in a heavy skillet and gently sauté the onion and garlic until translucent. Allow to cool. Combine the onion and garlic with the avocado, mozzarella, feta, olives, green onion, and dill. Season to taste with salt and pepper. Set aside.

Unfold a sheet of puff pastry and carefully cut into 3-inch squares. Baste the outer edges of each square with egg wash. Place a teaspoonful of the avocado mixture in the center of each square. Fold over to form a triangle. Using the tines of a fork, crimp the edges to seal well. Place about ½ inch apart on a parchment-lined baking sheet. Brush with additional egg wash. Using a small sharp knife, make 2 small slits in the top of each triangle. Bake for 20–25 minutes or until golden brown. Serve hot or cold.

Makes about 2 dozen

2 tablespoons olive oil

1 medium yellow onion, chopped

4–6 cloves garlic, minced

2 avocados, diced

1 cup grated mozzarella cheese

½ cup crumbled feta cheese

3–4 tablespoons chopped black olives

1 green onion, chopped, including most of the green top

1 tablespoon finely chopped fresh dill weed

Salt and freshly ground black pepper

1 package frozen puff pastry, thawed

Egg wash (1 egg beaten with 1 tablespoon cold water)

Avocado-Stuffed Mushrooms

xxxxxx

Here's a distinctive variation on the classic appetizer.

Makes about 20

Preheat the oven to broil.

Remove the mushroom stems and discard. Place the mushroom cups into boiling water and blanch for 2 minutes. Rinse under cold running water and set aside to drain.

Gently combine the crabmeat, olives, garlic, Gruyère and Cheddar cheeses, and avocado in a bowl, being careful not to overblend. Add salt and pepper to taste. Fill the blanched and drained mushroom cups with this mixture. Cut the bacon into thin slivers and lay several small strips across the top of each filled mushroom. Place under the broiler just until the bacon is crisp. Serve hot.

20 or so large
white mushrooms

1 can (6 ounces)
crabmeat, drained

2 tablespoons chopped
black olives

1 clove garlic,
very finely minced

$2/3$ cup grated Gruyère

$2/3$ cup grated
extra-sharp white Cheddar

1 large avocado,
diced very small

Salt and freshly
ground black pepper

1–2 strips of
thin-sliced bacon

La Californie (Avocado and Garlic Soup)

xxxxxx

I first had this soup in a small restaurant near the Palace of the Dauphine in Dijon. I was told the chef chose the name after he lived in California for a few years and grew to love avocados— and he much preferred California avocados over any others.

Roughly chop the garlic and place into a blender with the mustard and 1 cup of chicken stock. Blend until smooth. Add the avocados to the blender and process until smooth. Strain into a bowl.

Add the remaining stock, nutmeg, and cream. Stir well, season to taste with salt and pepper, and chill before serving. Serve in individual bowls with a garnish of sour cream, some clipped chives, and a few wedges of lime.

A lighter variation (serves 4) Combine half the chicken broth with 2 mashed avocados and 2–3 cloves roasted garlic (see page 16) in a blender until pureed. Add remaining broth, 1 cup half-and-half, ¼ cup cream Sherry, and salt and pepper to taste. Serve hot or chilled.

Serves 4–6

4–6 cloves roasted garlic
(see page 16)

1 tablespoon Sweet
and Hot Brown Mustard
(recipe follows)

4 cups or 2 cans
(15 ounces each) de-fatted
chicken broth

3 large avocados, mashed

1/2 teaspoon nutmeg

2 cups heavy cream

Salt and freshly
ground black pepper

Sour cream, for garnish

Fresh chives, for garnish

Lime wedges, for garnish

SWEET AND HOT BROWN MUSTARD

Pulse the brown and yellow mustard seeds in the blender until they are cracked but not pulverized. Combine them in a bowl with the mustard powder and sugar, then add cider vinegar and mix until you get a thin paste. Do not use this mustard for 2–3 days—it needs time to mellow, and the longer it sits the better it gets. This need not be refrigerated and will last indefinitely on your pantry shelf. If it thickens, just add more vinegar.

Makes about 3 cups

1/2 cup brown mustard seeds

1/2 cup yellow mustard seeds

1 cup dry yellow mustard
powder

2/3 cup sugar

Cider vinegar

Avocado and Seafood Soup

xxxxxx

Serves 4

4 cups or 2 (15-ounce) cans de-fatted chicken or fish stock

1 avocado, mashed

3–4 cloves garlic, chopped

2 avocados, diced

1 cup fresh chunky style salsa, hot or mild

2 cups pre-cooked shrimp, crabmeat, scallops, or other favorite cooked seafood

1/4 cup chopped fresh cilantro (reserve a few sprigs for garnish)

Salt and freshly ground black pepper

Lime slices, for garnish

I first had this delectable soup in a small open-air restaurant right on the beach in Veracruz. It is delicious and oh-so-easy to make.

Place 1 cup of the stock, the mashed avocado, and the garlic in a blender and process until smooth. If too thick, add a bit more stock. Strain into a bowl.

Add the diced avocados (reserving a few bits for garnish), salsa, seafood, and cilantro; stir gently, season to taste with salt and pepper, and serve well chilled. Garnish each serving with a sprig of fresh cilantro, a slice of lime, and a scattering of diced avocado.

Thai Avocado Seafood Soup

xxxxxx

For something flavorful and unique, give this one a try. You can make it as hot or as mild as you wish.

Place the noodles in a bowl and cover with boiling water. Allow to stand while you continue preparing the soup.

Shell and devein the prawns. Set aside the meat and place the shells in a large heavy pot along with the chicken broth, onion, garlic, gingerroot, fish, five-spice powder, soy sauce, sugar, and crushed chile pepper. Bring to a boil, reduce heat and simmer for 20–30 minutes. Allow to cool slightly, then strain, discarding the solids, and return the liquid to the pot.

Heat the oil in a heavy skillet. Gently sauté the scallops and prawns over medium heat until the prawns are pink and the scallops opaque, about 3–5 minutes. Remove from the pan and set aside. Add the bell pepper and gently sauté for 1–2 minutes, or until hot through. Set aside with the prawns and scallops. Drain the noodles.

To assemble, place the noodles in a large serving bowl. Scatter the prawns, scallops, and bell pepper over the noodles. Add the diced avocado and sprinkle with chopped cilantro to taste. Season the strained broth to taste with salt and pepper and bring back to a simmer. Ladle the hot liquid over the ingredients in the bowl, scatter several thin slices of fresh lime on top, and serve. This soup may also be served chilled.

Serves 4–6

1 ounce uncooked Oriental cellophane noodles

1/2 pound prawns

6 cups chicken broth

1 large onion, coarsely chopped

4–6 cloves garlic, chopped

1–2 thin slices fresh gingerroot

1 boneless fillet mild white fish (sole, turbot, cod, butterfish, or bass)

1 teaspoon Chinese five-spice powder

1/4 cup soy sauce

1 tablespoon sugar

Pinch of crushed chile pepper, or to taste

2 tablespoons peanut or olive oil

1/2 pound scallops

1/2 cup thinly slivered red bell pepper

2 large avocados, diced

Chopped fresh cilantro

Salt and freshly ground black pepper

1 lime, sliced

Grilled Chicken and Avocado Soup

xxxxx

Serves 4–6

4 cups chicken broth

4–6 cloves garlic, chopped

1 large onion, chopped

1 bay leaf

1 tablespoon Italian seasoning

2 boneless chicken breasts

6–8 cloves roasted garlic (see page 16)

Salt and freshly ground black pepper

2 large avocados, peeled and diced

1 cup garlic croutons

Chopped parsley

Don't be put off by the amount of garlic in this soup. The combination of fresh and roasted garlic is just right.

Put the chicken broth, chopped garlic, onion, bay leaf, and Italian seasoning into a large pot; bring to a boil, reduce heat, and simmer 20–30 minutes. Cool slightly, then strain.

Rinse the chicken breasts and pat dry. Mince the roasted garlic to a paste and spread on the chicken, kneading it a bit to work into the meat. Season to taste with salt and pepper, and grill or broil to desired degree of doneness, turning once. Cut into the thickest part with a small sharp knife; it is done when the meat is opaque instead of translucent.

Remove to a cutting surface and allow to rest for 5 minutes before slicing. Meanwhile, reheat the strained broth. Cut the chicken into very thin slivers and add to the soup. Add the diced avocados. Pour into a serving bowl and scatter the croutons and parsley over the top. Serve hot.

Chile and Cheese Avocado Soup

xxxxxx

Rich and satisfying, this soup can make a meal when served with fresh warm bread or tortillas.

Heat the olive oil in a heavy skillet over moderate heat and gently sauté the onion rings, garlic, and jalapeño until the onion is soft and translucent and just beginning to brown.

Place in a large pot with the broth and salsa and bring to a boil. Remove from heat and stir in the avocado and cilantro. Season to taste with salt and pepper. Ladle into serving bowls and sprinkle Cheddar and ricotta cheeses over the top. Garnish each bowl with a sprig of fresh cilantro and a wedge of lime.

Serves 4–6

2 tablespoons olive oil

1 medium-size yellow onion, sliced into thin rings

4–6 cloves garlic, minced

1 small jalapeño chile, seeded and cut into thin rings

6 cups chicken broth

1 cup chunky-style fresh salsa, hot or mild

2 large avocados, diced

$1/_4$ cup chopped fresh cilantro

Salt and freshly ground black pepper

1 cup grated extra-sharp Cheddar cheese

1 cup ricotta cheese, crumbled

Cilantro sprigs, for garnish

Lime wedge, for garnish

Avocado and Almond Soup

xxxxx

Serves 4–6

2 cloves roasted garlic (see page 16), finely minced

2 large, ripe avocados, mashed

$1/2$ teaspoon ground nutmeg

1 tablespoon finely minced fresh dill weed

4 cups chicken broth

$1/2$ cup almond flour

1 cup whipping cream

$1/4$ cup cream Sherry

Salt and freshly ground black pepper

Sour cream, for garnish

Fresh dill weed, for garnish

Almond flour is available in some specialty markets. If you can't find it, put roasted almonds into your blender or food processor and pulse until they are powdery. Be careful not to turn them into butter.

Place the garlic, mashed avocados, nutmeg, dill weed, and about 2 cups of broth in a blender and process until smooth. Put into a heavy pot with the remaining broth and bring to a boil. Reduce heat and simmer for 15–20 minutes.

Add the almond flour, cream, and Sherry, and heat to serving temperature, whisking to blend. Season to taste with salt and pepper. Garnish each serving with a dollop of sour cream and a sprig of fresh dill weed.

Gazpacho

xxxxxx

Gazpacho originated in Spain, yet every culture with a Mediterranean climate claims it as its own. I have had it in Spain, Portugal, Italy, Provence, and Mexico. Of course any trendy California café worth its chilled Chardonnay has a version on the menu, usually made with canned diced tomatoes. Here is a delicious, yet simple, version of a classic.

Put the tomato juice, broth, Sherry, tomatoes, cucumber, green onions, garlic, avocados, cilantro, dill, olives, and olive oil into a large bowl and stir gently to mix. Season to taste with salt and pepper and float the cucumber, purple onion, and lime or lemon garnishes on top. Serve ice cold.

Serves 6–8

4 cups tomato juice

2 cups beef broth

$1/2$ cup cream Sherry

2 ripe tomatoes, diced

$1/2$ cucumber, peeled and diced

2 green onions, chopped, including green tops

2–4 cloves garlic, very finely minced

2 avocados, diced

$1/4$ cup chopped fresh cilantro

2 tablespoons minced fresh dill weed

1 can ($2 1/4$ ounces) sliced black olives, drained

2–3 tablespoons olive oil

Salt and freshly ground black pepper

Several thin slices of unpeeled cucumber, for garnish

2–3 thin slices of sweet purple onion, separated into rings, for garnish

Several thin slices of fresh lime or lemon, for garnish

The Californian

xxxxx

Serves 4–6

3–4 thin slices of sweet purple onion, divided into rings

2 navel oranges, peeled, divided into segments, and diced

1 rib celery, diced

2 ripe yet firm avocados, diced

3 cups fresh crabmeat

1 cup frozen peas

2 tablespoons minced fresh dill weed

1 tablespoon minced fresh mint leaves

Curls of fresh Parmesan

Salt and freshly ground black pepper

2 heads crisp, fresh romaine lettuce

2–3 cloves roasted garlic (see page 16)

1 tablespoon Sweet and Hot Brown Mustard (see page 23)

$1/3$ cup aged balsamic vinegar

$1/4$ cup olive oil

2 avocados, sliced, for garnish

2 navel oranges, sliced into thin rings, for garnish

Sprigs of fresh mint or dill weed, for garnish

The following easy-to-make salad is the absolute epitome of California cuisine. It offers a delectable adventure for winter tables, since the three major ingredients—avocados, Dungeness crab and sweet, seedless navel oranges—are all at their peak in the winter months. If you don't have access to Dungeness crab, any crab will do. I've never met a crab I didn't like.

Very lightly toss the onion, orange segments, celery, avocado, crabmeat, peas, dill, mint, and Parmesan, with salt and pepper to taste. Line a serving plate with romaine leaves and pile the salad onto them.

In a small bowl, mash the roasted garlic and add the mustard, vinegar, and olive oil to make the dressing. Mix well and set aside.

Arrange the avocado and orange slices around the outer edge of the plate and intersperse with sprigs of fresh mint or dill. Drizzle the dressing over all and serve chilled. This is a superb salad to accompany an elegant meal—or an elegant meal on its own. Accompany with a good Chardonnay or pale ale and fresh baguette.

Summer Garden Salad

xxxxxx

If chunk Parmesan is not available, you may scatter grated Parmesan over the top to taste.

To make the dressing, combine the garlic, dill, cilantro, olive oil, vinegar, sugar, and Worcestershire sauce; mix well and set aside.

Peel the cucumber and remove the ends, then cut into thin slices. Cut half the onion into dice and the other half into thin slices, separating the rings. Halve and peel the avocados and cut into cross-wise (the short way) slices. Tear the lettuce into bite-size pieces. Combine the cucumber, purple onion, avocados, lettuce, tomatoes, celery, green onions, and red and yellow bell peppers in a salad bowl.

Mix the dressing again and pour over the salad. Toss gently. Season to taste with salt and pepper. Using a vegetable peeler, remove curls from a chunk of Parmesan cheese and scatter over the top of the salad.

Serves 4–6

2–3 cloves garlic, very finely minced

1 tablespoon minced fresh dill weed

2 tablespoons chopped fresh cilantro (optional)

$1/4$ cup olive oil

$1/2$ cup red wine vinegar

1 teaspoon sugar

1 teaspoon Worcestershire sauce

1 cucumber

1 medium-size sweet purple onion, peeled

2 large ripe avocados

4–6 leaves of crisp lettuce, such as Romaine or iceberg

2 large ripe tomatoes, cut into wedges

1 rib celery, cut into thin slices on the diagonal

2 green onions, cut into thin rings, including most of the green tops

1 red bell pepper, seeded and julienned

1 yellow bell pepper, seeded and julienned

Salt and freshly ground black pepper

Parmesan cheese

Avocado and Citrus Salad

XXXXX

Serves 4–6

1 can mandarin orange segments

1/4 cup olive oil

1/2 cup cider vinegar

1 tablespoon Sweet and Hot Brown Mustard (see page 23)

1 tablespoon finely chopped fresh dill weed

2 large navel oranges

1 pink grapefruit

1 sweet purple onion, peeled

2 avocados, diced

Salt and freshly ground black pepper

1 head of crisp lettuce, such as romaine

For special occasions, I often arrange slices of orange and avocado around the outer edge of this dish. This salad is also excellent with the addition of a cup or two of diced grilled chicken breast, shrimp, or crabmeat.

Drain the mandarin oranges and set them aside, reserving the juices. Combine this juice with the olive oil, vinegar, mustard, and dill, blending well to make dressing.

Peel the oranges and grapefruit and remove all the white pith. Separate into segments and cut into bite-size chunks. Slice half the onion into thin rings and dice the other half. Place the navel oranges, grapefruit, mandarin oranges, diced onion, and avocados in a bowl. Stir the dressing and pour it over the salad. Toss gently. Season to taste with salt and pepper. Line a serving dish with crisp lettuce and pile the salad in the center. Scatter the separated onion rings over the top.

Seafood and Avocado Salad

xxxxxx

Serves 4–6

1 tablespoon Sweet and Hot Brown Mustard (see page 23)

3 tablespoons olive oil

1/3 cup cider vinegar

1–2 cloves garlic, very finely minced

1 teaspoon sugar

1 tablespoon olive oil

2 tablespoons cream Sherry

2–3 cloves garlic, very finely minced

1/2 pound scallops

2 ounces uncooked small shell pasta

1/2 pound cooked baby shrimp

3 ripe avocados, diced

1 small sweet purple onion, diced

1 green onion, cut into thin rings, including most of the green tops

1 cup thinly sliced celery

1 tablespoon finely chopped fresh dill weed

Salt and freshly ground black pepper

Crisp lettuce leaves

This may be used as a side salad, but it also makes an excellent lunch or light dinner dish.

For the dressing, combine the mustard, 3 tablespoons of olive oil, vinegar, 1–2 minced garlic cloves, and sugar; blend well and set aside.

Heat the remaining tablespoon of olive oil in a heavy skillet with the Sherry. Over low heat, lightly sauté the remaining minced garlic until soft and translucent but not yet beginning to brown. Add the scallops and sauté until they are opaque, about 2–3 minutes. Set aside to cool.

Cook the pasta according to package directions. Rinse under cold running water and drain well. Place the pasta in a large bowl with the scallops, shrimp, avocados, onions, celery, and dill.

Pour the dressing over the ingredients in the bowl. Toss gently and season to taste with salt and pepper. Line individual serving plates with lettuce leaves, pile the salad over them, and serve.

Chicken Salad-Stuffed Avocados

xxxxxx

Here is an excellent recipe to make when you have leftover roasted, baked, or grilled chicken. You can also replace the cooked chicken with baby shrimp, crabmeat, or diced ham. Or for a wonderful vegetarian version, replace the chicken with a cup of diced, marinated, grilled tofu.

For the dressing, combine the mayonnaise, mustard, and garlic; mix well and set aside.

Combine the chicken, purple onion, red pepper, green onion, celery, dill, and cilantro in a bowl. Add the dressing and toss gently. Season to taste with salt and pepper. Lay a crisp leaf of lettuce on each of 4 plates. Cut the lime or lemon in half and gently rub it over the surface of the avocados to retard browning. Place an avocado half on each plate. Fill the avocados to overflowing with the salad. Garnish with sprigs of fresh mint and slices of lime or lemon.

Serves 4

1 cup mayonnaise

1 tablespoon Sweet and Hot Brown Mustard (see page 23)

3–4 cloves roasted garlic (see page 16), minced

2 cups cooked chicken, diced

$1/2$ medium-size sweet purple onion, diced

$1/2$ small sweet red bell pepper, diced

1 green onion, chopped small, including most of the green top

$1/2$ cup diced celery

1 teaspoon minced fresh dill weed

1 tablespoon minced fresh cilantro

Salt and freshly ground black pepper

4 crisp lettuce leaves

1 fresh lime or lemon

2 large, ripe avocados, halved

Fresh mint leaves, for garnish

4 slices lemon or lime, for garnish

Roasted Pepper and Avocado Salad

xxxxxx

Serves 4–6

With colorful peppers and onion, this recipe pleases the eye as well as the palate.

3 tablespoons olive oil

1/3 cup red wine vinegar

4–6 cloves roasted garlic (see page 16), minced

1 teaspoon sugar

1 roasted red bell pepper (see page 14)

1 roasted orange bell pepper (see page 14)

1 roasted yellow bell pepper (see page 14)

1 small sweet purple onion, cut into thin rings

1 can (6 ounces) whole pitted ripe olives, drained

1 tablespoon chopped fresh dill weed

1 cup crumbled feta cheese

2 avocados, diced

Salt and freshly ground black pepper

Crisp lettuce leaves

Mix the olive oil, vinegar, garlic, and sugar together well and set aside. Remove the seeds from the 3 roasted peppers and julienne. Put the onion rings into a bowl with the roasted peppers, olives, dill, feta, and avocados. Pour the dressing over all, toss gently, and season to taste with salt and pepper. Line a serving dish with crisp lettuce leaves and pile the salad in the middle.

Avocado, Walnut, and Chicken Salad

xxxxxx

A luscious West Coast salad with hints of the Mediterranean.

Serves 4–6

Put the sour cream, buttermilk, tahini, garlic, and sugar into a blender and process to make the dressing. Taste and adjust the seasonings with sesame oil and salt. Set aside.

Heat the olive oil in a heavy skillet and lightly toast the walnut pieces. Set aside to cool. Put the peas in a colander and pour boiling water over them. Set aside to cool. Peel the oranges and remove all the pith. Pull into segments and cut into ½-inch pieces. Slice the chicken breasts into thin slivers. Combine the walnuts, peas, oranges, avocados, celery, onion, and chicken in a large bowl. Add the dressing and toss lightly. Season to taste with salt and pepper. Line individual salad plates with the lettuce mix. Put generous helpings of the salad on each plate and serve chilled.

½ cup sour cream

½ cup buttermilk

4 tablespoons tahini

3–4 cloves roasted garlic (see page 16)

1 teaspoon sugar

Sesame oil

Salt

1 tablespoon olive oil

Generous ½ cup chopped walnuts

1 cup frozen peas

2 navel oranges

2 grilled chicken breasts

2 large ripe avocados, diced

2 ribs celery, diced

½ medium-size sweet purple onion, diced

Salt and freshly ground black pepper

Caesar salad lettuce mix or torn leaves of crisp romaine

Avocado and Berry Salad

xxxxxx

This is an excellent salad to serve with grilled chicken breasts or grilled pork—or try it as a refreshing dessert.

Serves 4–6

Blend the olive oil, blackberry and balsamic vinegars, and Dijon mustard together for the dressing and set aside. Stem the strawberries and cut in half. (Reserve a few whole ones with stems to use as garnish.) Put all the berries, avocados, mint, and dill in a bowl and add the dressing. Toss gently. Place radicchio leaves on individual serving plates and divide the salad among them. Place 2 or 3 sesame crackers on the side of each plate and lay a small slice of blue cheese on them. Give the salad a few grindings of black pepper and serve chilled.

$1/4$ cup olive oil

$1/3$ cup blackberry vinegar

2 tablespoons
balsamic vinegar

1 teaspoon Dijon mustard

2 cups strawberries

1 cup blackberries, rinsed

1 cup blueberries, rinsed

2 avocados, diced

2 tablespoons finely chopped
fresh mint leaves

1 tablespoon finely chopped
fresh dill weed

Radicchio leaves
(or substitute curly endive
or frisée)

Sesame crackers

Blue cheese

Freshly ground
black pepper

Christmas Salad

xxxxxx

Serves 6–8 *This makes a beautiful addition to your Christmas table.*

1 cup sour cream

2 tablespoons Sweet and Hot Brown Mustard (see page 23)

2 tablespoons frozen orange juice concentrate

1 tablespoon whole-berry cranberry sauce

1/4 cup cream Sherry

1 teaspoon dill weed

3–4 navel oranges

1 small jicama

2–3 Fuji apples

2–3 pears

2–3 ripe persimmons

3–4 avocados

Juice of 2–3 fresh limes

Curly endive

About 1/2 cup pomegranate seeds

Sprigs of fresh mint, for garnish

Put the sour cream, mustard, orange juice concentrate, cranberry sauce, Sherry, and dill into the jar of your blender and puree for the dressing. Set aside. Peel the oranges, remove all of the white pith, and cut into ¼-inch slices. Peel the jicama and cut into sticks about ¼ x ½ x 3 inches. Core the apples and cut into thin wedges. Core the pears, unpeeled, and cut into strips. Cut the persimmons into rounds; do not peel. Peel and slice the avocados. Sprinkle the jicama, apples, pears, and avocados with lime juice to retard browning.

Line a large serving platter with the curly endive. Place the prepared fruit pieces on the platter in alternate rows. Stir the dressing and drizzle it over the cut fruits. Scatter the pomegranate seeds over all and garnish with sprigs of fresh mint.

Avocado Quiche

xxxxxx

Makes an 8- to 9-inch quiche

4 strips bacon, diced

Olive oil

1 medium-size yellow onion, diced

4–6 cloves garlic, minced

About 2 cups thinly sliced mushrooms

1 teaspoon Italian seasoning (or equivalent in favorite fresh herbs)

1/2 cup grated extra-sharp white Cheddar

1/2 cup grated Gruyère, Emmentaler, or other good Swiss cheese

1/2 cup grated Parmesan

1 tablespoon cornstarch

1/4 cup chopped fresh parsley

1 large ripe avocado, mashed

2 eggs, beaten

2 cups milk or half-and-half

1/2 teaspoon nutmeg

Salt and freshly ground black pepper

1 prepared pie shell, chilled (make your own or buy a frozen one)

This may be eaten warm or cold. I think quiche is usually better the day after it is baked. Serve with a small dollop of sour cream. For some easy variations, try replacing the sautéed bacon with any of the following: 1 cup slivered ham, 1 cup flaked crabmeat, 1 cup chopped baby shrimp meat, or 1/2 cup slivered prosciutto.

Preheat oven to 350 degrees F. Fry the diced bacon in a heavy skillet over moderate heat until crisp but not hard. Remove with a slotted spoon and set aside. Pour off the fat. Add a bit of olive oil and gently sauté the onion and garlic, just until softened. Add the mushrooms and sauté until soft and translucent but not yet beginning to brown. Add Italian seasoning or herbs and continue to sauté for another minute or so. Remove everything with a slotted spoon and set aside with the bacon.

Toss the Cheddar, Swiss, and Parmesan cheeses together with the cornstarch and parsley and set aside.

Beat the avocado, eggs, and milk together; add the nutmeg and salt and pepper to taste.

When the mushroom mixture is completely cooled, place it in the pie shell in alternate layers with the cheeses, reserving about 1/4 of cheese. Place the pie plate in a larger ovenproof dish and place on the center rack of the oven. Pour in the avocado mixture and sprinkle the top with the remaining cheese. Add water to the larger baking dish to create a water bath. Bake for 45–60 minutes or until a skewer inserted in the center comes out clean. Remove from the oven and allow to sit for a bit before slicing.

Avocado and Crab–Stuffed Ravioli

xxxxxx

This cooking adventure leads to something really special—little pillows of dough filled with flavor.

For the ravioli pasta, mix the flour, 1 tablespoon of oil, and 1 egg together in a bowl. Add just enough water to form into a soft dough. Mix well, turn out onto a lightly floured surface, and knead extremely well. Put it back in the bowl, cover, and allow to rest while you make the filling.

Heat 1–2 tablespoons of olive oil in a heavy skillet and gently sauté the yellow onion and 3–4 cloves of minced garlic until the onion is translucent and just beginning to brown around the edges. Remove to a bowl and mix in the green onion, Gruyère, ricotta, olives, avocado, nutmeg, and salt and pepper to taste. Set aside.

For the sauce, heat the butter and Sherry together in a heavy skillet and gently sauté the remaining minced garlic until it is soft. Add the cream, nutmeg, dill, and cayenne and bring to a boil. Reduce the heat to a simmer and continue to cook until the sauce has thickened and is reduced by about one third. Season to taste with salt and pepper.

To assemble the ravioli, divide the dough into 2 or 4 pieces. On a lightly floured surface, roll out into a rectangle approximately ⅛ inch thick. Using a pastry wheel or a sharp knife, cut the dough into approximately 1½-inch squares. Paint the outer edges of half the squares with egg wash. Place a spoonful of the filling in the center of each of the squares that have been

Serves 4

1½ cups all-purpose flour

1 tablespoon olive oil

1 egg, lightly beaten

Cold water

1–2 tablespoons olive oil

1 medium-size yellow onion, finely chopped

3–4 cloves garlic, minced

1 green onion, minced, including most of the green top

½ cup Gruyère cheese, grated (or other good Swiss cheese)

½ cup ricotta

2 tablespoons chopped black olives

1 large ripe avocado, diced small

½ teaspoon grated nutmeg

Salt and freshly ground black pepper

4 tablespoons (½ stick) butter

¼ cup cream Sherry

3–4 cloves garlic, minced

½ cup whipping cream

Pinch of grated nutmeg

Pinch of dill weed

Pinch of cayenne pepper

(ingredients continue on next page)

Salt and freshly
ground black pepper

Egg wash (1 egg
beaten with 1
tablespoon cold water)

1/2 cup grated fresh
Parmesan

Chopped fresh parsley,
for garnish

Chopped black olives,
for garnish

painted with the egg wash. Place a second square of dough on top of each of the filled squares and pinch all the way around the outer edges to seal well. Set aside and continue rolling and filling the dough until you run out of either dough or filling.

Carefully slide the finished ravioli into a large pot of gently boiling water and poach for about 4–5 minutes, or to your desired degree of doneness. When they are done, lift the ravioli from the pot with a slotted spoon and place them in the skillet of sauce. Reheat the sauce and gently fold in the Parmesan. Place on a serving platter and garnish with a sprinkling of fresh parsley and chopped black olives.

Pasta in No-Cook Sauce

xxxxxx

This dish should not be thought of as a pasta salad. It is a pasta entrée with an uncooked sauce. It's easy, quick, and absolutely delicious. And please, don't be put off by the use of anchovies. They do not permeate the dish. They just give it depth. Rigatoni, penne, orrechiette, twists, bowties, and medium shells are all good shapes to use for this dish.

Put the mustard, garlic, olive oil, vinegar, anchovies, green and purple onions, capers, and basil into a large serving bowl and mix well. Bring a large pot of water to a boil and add the pasta. Cook to the al dente stage, then drain but do not rinse. Add to the bowl. Add the tomatoes, avocados, piñon nuts, and Parmesan and toss gently. Season to taste with salt and pepper. Serve while still hot.

Serves 4–6

2 tablespoons Sweet and Hot Brown Mustard (see page 23)

6–8 cloves roasted garlic (see page 16), minced

1/4 cup olive oil

1/4 cup cider vinegar

2 anchovy fillets, minced

2 green onions, chopped very small, including most of the green tops

1 small sweet purple onion, diced small

2 tablespoons capers, rinsed

1/4 cup finely chopped fresh basil

10–12 ounces uncooked pasta

About 1 cup halved small cherry tomatoes

2 large avocados, diced

1/2 cup shelled piñon nuts

1/2 cup freshly grated Parmesan cheese

Salt and freshly ground black pepper

Pasta with Avocados and Grilled Chicken Breasts

xxxxxx

Serves 4–6

10–12 ounces uncooked linguine or fettuccini

2 tablespoons olive oil

6–8 cloves roasted garlic (see page 16), minced

1 tablespoon Sweet and Hot Brown Mustard (see page 23)

2 cups whipping cream

1 large tomato, diced

2 avocados, diced

2 grilled chicken breasts, diced

$1/2$ cup grated fresh Parmesan cheese

$1/4$ cup chopped fresh parsley

Salt and freshly ground black pepper

Parsley sprigs, for garnish

Light yet rich—perfect for the eating habits of the twenty-first century.

Bring a large pot of water to a boil. Add the pasta and cook to the al dente stage; drain, return to the pot, and gently stir in the olive oil. Put the garlic and mustard in a heavy skillet and blend together over moderate heat. Add the cream, bring to a boil, reduce heat to medium, and whisk constantly until reduced by about a third (about 3–4 minutes). Add the tomato and cook for another minute or so. Add the avocados and chicken and stir gently, cooking only until heated through. Pour this over the pasta. Add the Parmesan and parsley and season to taste with salt and pepper. Put into a serving dish and garnish with sprigs of fresh parsley.

Rigatoni with Avocado, Olives, and Roasted Peppers

xxxxxx

This fusion recipe blends California roots with Mediterranean heritage.

Bring a large pot of water to a boil, add the rigatoni and cook to the al dente stage. Drain but do not rinse. Return to the pot and gently stir in the 1–2 tablespoons of olive oil.

Heat the additional 2 tablespoons of olive oil in a large skillet and gently sauté the onion and garlic with the Italian seasoning until the onions are translucent and just beginning to brown around the edges. Add the peppers, green onions, and olives and sauté for another minute or so. Add the avocados and toss gently for about a minute or until heated. Put the pasta into a large serving bowl, then add the pepper and avocado mixture, Parmesan, and parsley. Toss gently and season to taste with salt and pepper. You may wish to drizzle on a bit more olive oil.

Serves 4–6

10–12 ounces uncooked rigatoni

1–2 tablespoons olive oil

2 tablespoons additional olive oil

1 medium-size yellow onion, diced

4–6 cloves garlic, minced

1 teaspoon Italian seasoning

2 roasted bell peppers (see page 14), seeded and diced

2 green onions, chopped, including most of the green tops

1 can (2 1/4 ounces) sliced black olives, drained

2 avocados, diced

1/2 cup freshly grated Parmesan cheese

1/4 cup chopped fresh parsley

Salt and freshly ground black pepper

California Omelette

xxxxx

Serves 1

2 large eggs

1 tablespoon olive oil

1/4 medium-size yellow onion, diced

1–2 cloves garlic, minced

1/4 cup diced celery

1/2 teaspoon Italian seasoning

1/4 cup grated extra-sharp Cheddar

1/4 cup grated aged Gruyère or other good-quality Swiss cheese

1/2 cup flaked crabmeat

1/2 diced avocado

2 tablespoons chopped black olives

About 2 tablespoons diced roasted pepper (see page 14)

Salt and freshly ground black pepper

3 tablespoons butter

1/4 cup cream Sherry

1 tablespoon minced fresh dill weed (or pinch of dry)

Pinch of nutmeg

Sour cream

Sprigs of fresh dill weed

Slice of fresh lime or lemon

I realize that most people tend to think of omelettes as a break-fast food only. Phooey! Give them a try for dinner as well. They're not only delicious but very easy, and their infinite variety is limited only by your imagination. If you are making more than one omelette, sauté all the vegetables at one time. Roasted peppers come in vinegar, oil, or water—use the oil or water pack. Or you can make your own (see page 14).

Beat the eggs in a small bowl and allow to sit while you prepare the other ingredients. Heat the olive oil in a heavy skillet and gently sauté the onion, garlic, celery, and Italian seasoning together until the onion and celery are soft and translucent and only just beginning to become golden brown around the edges. Remove to a bowl and set aside.

Wipe an 8-inch nonstick skillet or omelette pan with a bit of olive oil and put the skillet over medium heat. Test for proper heat by putting a few drops of the beaten egg into it. If they gently become firm in about a second without sizzling or curling around the edges, the pan is the correct temperature. Gently pour the eggs into the skillet and allow to sit undisturbed until a thin skin has formed on the bottom but most of the egg is still liquid, about 1 minute.

Sprinkle the Cheddar and Gruyère cheeses over the surface, and with the back of a table fork, gently agitate the surface until the cheese and egg are incorporated, being careful not to break the skin on the bottom. Before the egg is completely set, sprinkle the cooked onion mixture, crabmeat, avocado, olives, and roasted pepper over the surface. Season to taste with salt and pepper. When the eggs are cooked to your liking, fold the omelette in half and turn off the heat. Allow it to sit in the hot pan for about 30 seconds more, then slide it onto a heated plate. Place in a warm oven while you make the sauce.

In a clean skillet, melt the butter with the Sherry and add the dill and nutmeg. Swirl together and allow to simmer for about 1 minute. Pour over the omelette. Add a generous dollop of sour cream and garnish with a sprig of dill weed and a slice of lemon or lime. Served with fresh baguette and a soft wine such as a Chignon Blanc, this makes an elegant lunch or dinner. Try it by candlelight in front of the fire some special evening.

Avocado Seafood Fondue

xxxxxx

Serves 2

1 tablespoon olive oil

About 1/2 cup diced yellow onion

1–2 cloves garlic, minced

1 cup grated Swiss cheese such as Gruyère or Emmentaler

1 cup grated extra-sharp white Cheddar

1 tablespoon cornstarch

1 cup Pilsner-style beer

1/2 teaspoon nutmeg

1 tablespoon minced fresh dill weed

1 cup flaked crabmeat or chopped baby shrimp

1 large ripe avocado, diced

2 tablespoons chopped black olives

2 tablespoons diced roasted red peppers (see page 14)

Salt and freshly ground black pepper

French bread cut into 1-inch cubes

This recipe may be increased to serve as many as you wish; however, in my opinion, the whole purpose of fondue is for two people to recline on cushions in front of a fire, feeding each other.

Heat the olive oil in a heavy skillet and gently sauté the onion and garlic until they are soft and translucent but not yet beginning to brown. Set aside. Combine the Swiss and Cheddar cheeses and toss together with the cornstarch. Put into a heavy pot with the beer, nutmeg, and dill. Gently whisk together over a low heat until the cheeses are melted and blended. Add the crab or shrimp, avocado, olives, roasted peppers, and salt and pepper to taste. Heat and pour into a fondue dish. Accompany with a basket of bread cubes, fondue forks, candlelight, wine, and someone special.

Avocado and Shrimp Pizza Alfredo

xxxxxx

This recipe uses a frozen pizza crust and commercially bottled Alfredo sauce, which is nice for cooks who are short on time— or just feeling lazy.

Preheat the oven as per the pizza crust directions. Place the crust on a baking sheet and spread with the roasted garlic. Cover the crust generously with Alfredo sauce. Toss the cheeses and parsley together and sprinkle about two-thirds of the mixture over the pizza. Scatter avocado, shrimp and artichoke hearts over this. Sprinkle with the remaining cheese mixture, season to taste with salt and pepper, and put into the preheated oven. Bake according to the package directions or until the cheese is bubbling and the crust is beginning to brown.

Serves 4

1 frozen pizza crust (12–14 inches)

6–8 cloves roasted garlic (see page 16), minced

1 jar Alfredo sauce

$1/2$ cup grated mozzarella

$1/2$ cup grated fresh Parmesan

$1/4$ cup chopped parsley

1 avocado, diced

$1/4$ pound cooked baby shrimp meat

3–4 water-packed artichoke hearts, diced

Salt and freshly grated pepper

Avocado, Ham, Roasted Pepper, and Olive Pizza

XXXXXX

Serves 3–4

1 frozen pizza crust (12–14 inches)

1 jar red Italian-style sauce

3–4 cloves garlic, very thinly sliced

1/3 cup grated extra-sharp Cheddar

1/3 cup grated mozzarella

1/3 cup freshly grated Parmesan

1/4 cup chopped fresh parsley

1 cup slivered ham

1/2 cup roasted pepper (see page 14), julienned

1 ripe avocado, diced

2–3 tablespoons chopped black olives

1 tablespoon capers

Salt and freshly ground black pepper

This recipe goes against my usual culinary ethics by using a commercially prepared pizza crust and bottled sauce. You may use a loaf of French bread split in half instead of a pizza crust if you wish.

Preheat the oven according to the directions for the pizza crust. Thaw the crust and place it on a baking pan. Spread with sauce and sprinkle with sliced garlic. Toss the Cheddar, mozzarella, Parmesan, and parsley together. Sprinkle about two-thirds of this mix over the crust. Then sprinkle the ham, roasted pepper, avocado, olives, and capers onto the pizza. Season to taste with salt and pepper and sprinkle on the remaining cheese mixture. Bake according to the crust directions, or until the cheeses are bubbling and the edges of the crust are browned. Serve hot.

Avocado and Seafood–Stuffed Giant Pasta Shells

xxxxxx

Serves 4

12 giant pasta shells

Olive oil

2 tablespoons olive oil

1 medium-size yellow onion, diced

4–6 cloves garlic, minced

2 cups whipping cream

1 tablespoon minced fresh dill weed

$1/2$ teaspoon grated nutmeg

1 cup freshly grated Parmesan

$1/4$ pound cooked baby shrimp (or 6 ounces canned crabmeat, drained, or combination thereof)

1 avocado, diced

$1/4$ cup chopped fresh parsley

Salt and freshly ground black pepper

Grated mozzarella cheese

Additional fresh parsley, for garnish

You may have to look around a bit to find giant pasta shells. They look just like the small and medium shells but are about 2½–3 inches long.

Put the pasta shells into a large pot of boiling water and cook to the al dente stage. Rinse under cold running water, draining well, then put into a bowl with a bit of olive oil to prevent sticking. Set aside.

Preheat the oven to 350 degrees F.

Heat the 2 tablespoons olive oil in a heavy skillet and gently sauté the onion and garlic until the onion is translucent but not yet beginning to brown. Add the cream, bring to a boil, reduce heat to a rapid simmer, and cook until the volume is reduced by about one third. Add the dill, nutmeg, Parmesan, seafood, avocado, and parsley. Season to taste with salt and pepper.

Set the shells in a baking pan just large enough to hold them comfortably. Fill the shells with the seafood mixture. If there is any left over, pour it over them. Sprinkle with some grated mozzarella and put in the center of the oven for 20–30 minutes or until the sauce is bubbling and the cheese melted. Gently remove the filled shells to a serving plate. Spoon any extra sauce from the baking dish over them, garnish with sprigs of fresh parsley, and serve hot.

Quick and Easy Avocado Fajitas

xxxxxx

Each may assemble his or her own fajita by scooping up some of the mixture and rolling it up in a flour tortilla.

Serves 4–6

Heat the olive oil in a large heavy skillet. Separate the onion into rings and gently sauté with the garlic until the onion is pinkish and translucent. Add the chicken breasts and continue to sauté until the meat is opaque instead of translucent. I like to let it brown slightly around the edges. Season with salt and pepper. Add the roasted pepper and sauté just until heated through. Add the salsa, avocados, and cilantro, and continue to cook over moderate heat until heated through. Season to taste with more salt and pepper. Serve with fresh warm flour tortillas, and offer sour cream and lime wedges for garnish.

1–2 tablespoons olive oil

1 large yellow onion, cut into thin slices

4–6 cloves garlic, sliced very thin

2 boneless chicken breasts, cut into thin strips

Salt and freshly ground black pepper

1 roasted bell pepper (see page 14), seeded and julienned

1 1/2 cups chunky-style salsa (mild or hot)

2 avocados, thinly sliced

1/4 cup chopped fresh cilantro

8–12 flour tortillas

Sour cream, for garnish

Fresh lime wedges, for garnish

Stuffed Chicken Breasts in Sesame Sauce

xxxxxx

Serves 4

4 boneless chicken breasts

Salt and freshly ground black pepper

6–8 cloves roasted garlic (see page 16), finely minced

1 cup grated Gruyère, Emmentaler, or other good Swiss cheese

1 large avocado, sliced

2 tablespoons butter

2 tablespoons olive oil

$1/4$ cup cream Sherry

$1/2$ cup tahini

2 cups whipping cream

$1/2$ teaspoon nutmeg

Sesame seeds, for garnish

Minced parsley, for garnish

Tahini, a Middle Eastern paste made from ground sesame seeds, forms the basis of this savory sauce.

Place the chicken breasts between sheets of plastic wrap and pound gently with a wooden kitchen mallet or rolling pin to flatten. Season each flattened breast with salt and pepper and spread with garlic. Sprinkle with grated cheese and top each breast with 2 or 3 slices of avocado. Form into a roll and secure with toothpicks. Heat the butter and oil in a heavy skillet and gently sauté the breasts to desired degree of doneness. They are done when the meat is opaque instead of translucent. Pour in Sherry and continue to sauté until the rolls are golden brown on all sides. Remove to a plate and set aside while you make the sauce.

Add tahini and about ½ cup of the cream to the skillet and whisk over moderate heat until smooth. Add the remaining cream and nutmeg and, whisking frequently, simmer rapidly until the volume is reduced by about one third. Season to taste with salt and pepper. Pour sauce over the chicken breasts and garnish with a sprinkling of sesame seeds and minced parsley.

Avocado Scramble

xxxxxx

This delectable scramble makes for an excellent breakfast or Sunday brunch, but think of it as a superb quick and easy lunch or dinner dish as well, especially when served with a full-bodied pale ale or nice crisp Chardonnay and a fresh baguette.

Heat the olive oil in a large heavy skillet. Gently sauté the yellow onion and garlic until the onions are translucent and just beginning to brown around the edges. Add green onions and continue to sauté for about another minute. Add the tomato, avocado, olives, capers, basil, dill, and parsley, and gently cook only until heated through. Beat the eggs with the cream and pour into the skillet with the vegetables. Sprinkle cheese over the top and season to taste with salt and pepper. Allow to sit undisturbed over moderate heat for a minute or so. Then, using a wooden spatula, gently pull the eggs from the opposite side of the skillet towards you and tip the pan so that the uncooked egg runs onto the skillet. Continue until all the egg is cooked to your liking.

I prefer my eggs a bit on the soft side, but many people like them quite dry. This is excellent served as is or with a bit of sour cream and salsa of choice.

Serves 4

2–3 tablespoons olive oil

1 medium-size yellow onion, diced

4–6 cloves garlic, minced

2 green onions, chopped, including most of the green tops

1 large tomato, diced

1 large avocado, diced

3 tablespoons chopped black olives

1 tablespoon capers, rinsed

2 tablespoons minced fresh basil

1 tablespoon minced fresh dill weed

$1/4$ cup chopped fresh parsley

8 eggs

$1/4$ cup whipping cream

1 cup grated cheese of choice

Salt and freshly ground black pepper

Avocado Crepes

XXXXXX

*Makes about
1 dozen 7-inch crepes*

¹/₂ cup all-purpose flour

¹/₂ cup milk

¹/₄ cup lukewarm water

2 eggs

2 tablespoons melted butter

1 teaspoon sugar

¹/₂ teaspoon nutmeg

Pinch of salt

Oil

1 tablespoon butter

1 tablespoon all-purpose flour

1¹/₂ cups milk, half-and-half, or whipping cream

¹/₂ cup grated Cheddar

¹/₂ cup grated mozzarella

¹/₂ teaspoon nutmeg

2–3 tablespoons chopped chives

Pinch of cayenne pepper

1 avocado, well mashed

Salt and freshly ground black pepper

Your choice of fillings (see headnote for ideas)

Additional grated cheese for topping

Many people are afraid to make crepes, but they aren't all that difficult. If your batter thickens, just add a bit more water. The easiest way to make beautiful thin crepes is to put a small ladle full of batter into the heated pan, swirl it around until the bottom of the pan is evenly coated, then pour any excess batter back into the mixing bowl. When the dough begins to set, you can cut off the little tail of batter that will be cooked onto the side of the pan. You may make your crepes several hours in advance if you wish. Just let them cool off completely, then wrap them loosely in plastic wrap and set aside until needed. Use any combination of these fillings: grated cheese (Cheddar, mozzarella, Gruyère, Emmentaler, ricotta, or feta), sautéed mushroom slices, flaked crabmeat, cooked baby shrimp, slivered grilled chicken breast, slivered cooked ham, crumbled bacon, chopped black olives, and chopped roasted red bell pepper (see page 14).

Put the ½ cup of flour, ½ cup of milk, water, eggs, 2 tablespoons of melted butter, sugar, ½ teaspoon nutmeg, and pinch of salt into your blender and process until well mixed, smooth, and creamy. Set aside and let it rest for about 30 minutes.

When ready to begin, wipe your pan with oil and place it over moderate heat. When the pan is properly heated, pour in a ladle full of batter and swirl to coat the bottom of the pan evenly. If you think there is a bit too much batter in the pan, just pour the excess back into the bowl. Allow the crepe to cook until, if you lift an edge and peek, it is a pale golden brown and all of the batter has set. At this point, flip the crepe over and continue cooking until the other side is a pale golden brown as well. I have always found it easiest to loosen around the edges with a spatula, then gingerly pick up an edge with my fingers and flip. You may stack the crepes on a plate and set aside. Wipe the pan with a bit more oil as needed between crepes and continue until all your batter is gone. Set the finished crepes aside while you make the sauce.

To make the sauce, heat the tablespoon of butter and tablespoon of flour together in a heavy pot and blend into a paste. Do not allow to brown. Gradually pour in the 1½ cups of milk, whisking all the while. Continue to whisk over low heat until thickened. Add the grated Cheddar and mozzarella, ½ teaspoon of nutmeg, chives, and cayenne. Whisk until the cheeses have melted. Add the mashed avocado, whisk, and season to taste with salt and pepper; set aside.

Preheat the oven to 350 degrees F.

Place all the selected fillings you will be using in individual bowls.

To assemble, lay a crepe on a flat surface in front of you. Spread it thinly with about a tablespoonful of sauce. Next sprinkle with whatever other fillings you are using. Roll the crepe up and place in a baking dish that may be served from. Continue in this manner until all the crepes have been used. Pour the remaining sauce over the rolled crepes, sprinkle the top lightly with grated cheese, and bake just until the cheese is melted and the top is barely beginning to brown. Garnish with sprigs of fresh parsley or dill and serve immediately.

Sandwiches and
Baked Goods

xxxxxx

The San Franciscan

xxxxxx

Avocado, Dungeness crab, and San Francisco sourdough bread—it doesn't get much more Californian than these ingredients. The following sandwich may seem a bit "trendy," as my English friends would say, but it is delectable and a perfect use of these wonderful California products.

Split the French roll or piece of baguette in half horizontally. Remove most of the soft bread from the bottom half. Lightly toast both halves. Mix cocktail sauce and mayonnaise together to taste and spread generously on both halves of the bread. Generously spread avocado on the bottom half, then fill with crabmeat. Sprinkle salt and pepper over the crab to taste (be generous with the pepper). Lay several slices of cheese on top of the crab and cover with thin slices of onion. Top with thinly sliced tomato and a generous amount of lettuce. Add the top half of the roll, pour yourself a glass of a chilled crisp white wine such as a Chignon Blanc or a good full-bodied Pilsner, and prepare to enjoy yourself.

Serves 1

1 large sourdough roll, or about 1/3 baguette

Favorite cocktail sauce

Favorite mayonnaise

1 ripe avocado, mashed

About 1/2 cup flaked crabmeat

Salt and freshly ground black pepper

Thinly sliced Swiss-type cheese (Gruyère and Emmentaler are both excellent)

Sweet purple onion rings

Tomato slices

Crisp lettuce (such as iceberg or romaine)

The Pompeii

xxxxxx

Serves 4

1 large flat round
loaf sourdough bread

Sweet and Hot Brown
Mustard (see page 23)

Mayonnaise

1–2 avocados, mashed

8–10 cloves roasted garlic
(see page 16), minced

3–4 tablespoons
chopped black olives

1 tablespoon capers, rinsed

1–2 peperoncini, chopped

Thinly sliced tomato

Thinly sliced sweet
purple onion

Thinly sliced prosciutto

Thinly sliced Swiss cheese

Salt and freshly
ground black pepper

This sandwich gets its name from the round, flat loaves of sourdough bread produced by some bakeries. One of my favorite bakeries calls theirs The Pompeii, after loaves of the same shape that archaeologists found preserved in a bakery in the ruins of that city.

Cut the loaf of bread in half horizontally so that you have two flat discs. Spread the bottom half with mustard and the top half with mayonnaise. Spread avocado generously over the bottom half, followed by the garlic, black olives, capers, and peperoncini. Cover with tomato slices and onion rings, then top with prosciutto and Swiss cheese. Season to taste with salt and pepper. Wrap loosely in plastic wrap and put on a flat surface. Put a large cutting board on top of it and set something heavy on the cutting board. Leave for 1–2 hours. To serve, cut into pie-shaped wedges.

One Burger Beyond

xxxxxx

Wear old clothes when you eat this, because you can't possibly bite into it without getting it all down your front. But oh is it worth the extra load of laundry!

Grill your beef patty to exactly the way you like it. Lightly toast the French roll. Mash the garlic and spread on one side of the roll, then spread with mustard and mayonnaise. Lay the beef patty on the bottom half, topping it with a slice of onion, followed by slices of avocado and tomato, and top with lettuce. Season to taste with salt and lots of freshly ground black pepper.

Serves 1

1 beef patty

1 large French roll, split

2–3 cloves roasted garlic (see page 16)

Sweet and Hot Brown Mustard (see page 23)

Mayonnaise

1 slice sweet purple onion

Avocado slices

Tomato slices

Crisp lettuce

Salt and freshly ground black pepper

Vegetarian Burger

xxxxxx

Serves 1

Portobellos offer a richer flavor and "meatier" texture than you find in smaller mushrooms.

1 large French roll

1 portobello mushroom

Olive oil

Several cloves roasted garlic
(see page 16)

Mayonnaise

Sweet and Hot Brown
Mustard (see page 23)

Sliced avocado

Roasted red bell
pepper (see page 14)

Sweet purple onion rings

Crisp lettuce

Salt and freshly
ground black pepper

Split and lightly toast a French roll. Cut a portobello mushroom crosswise into ¼-inch-thick "steaks," paint them with olive oil, and either grill or lightly fry them in a heavy skillet. Mince several cloves of roasted garlic to a paste and spread on one side of the roll, then spread with mayonnaise and mustard. Top with slices of portobello. Cover with slices of avocado, roasted pepper, onion rings, and lettuce. Season to taste with salt and pepper.

Avocado and Olive Sandwich Spread

xxxxxx

Makes about 1 cup

1 large, ripe
avocado, mashed

2–3 tablespoons
chopped black olives

2–3 cloves roasted garlic
(see page 16), minced

About 1/4 cup finely chopped
sweet purple onion

1 tablespoon capers, rinsed

Fresh lime juice

Salt and freshly
ground black pepper

*I like this best on either a toasted French roll with crisp lettuce
or on whole-grain bread with alfalfa sprouts.*

Mix all ingredients together well.

Avocado Cornbread

xxxxxx

Masa harina is the corn flour used to make tortillas and tamales. If you can't find it, use 1½ cups yellow cornmeal and 1½ cups all-purpose flour instead. On the ranch, my mother often served this bread with molasses.

Preheat the oven to 500 degrees F. Put the 2 tablespoons of oil in a 9- or 10-inch cast-iron skillet and put into the oven. Mix together the cornmeal, masa harina, flour, sugar, baking powder, and salt in a large bowl. Beat the oil and eggs together and add to the cornmeal mixture. Add as much cold water as needed to form a thick batter. Stir only until the ingredients are well incorporated. Fold in the avocado. Carefully remove the heated skillet from the oven and quickly pour the batter into it, getting the skillet back into the oven before it cools off. Bake at 500 degrees F for 5 minutes, then reduce the heat to 350 degrees F and bake for another 40–45 minutes or until a slim skewer inserted in the center comes out clean. Cut into wedges and serve with butter.

Variations For a chili and cheese cornbread, add 1 cup grated sharp Cheddar and 2 tablespoons of chili seasoning. Bake as directed above. For salsa cornbread, omit the water and add 1 cup of chunky-style fresh salsa and 1 cup of grated sharp Cheddar cheese. Bake as directed above. You may also pour the batter into oiled muffin tins instead of the skillet, and bake for about 30–35 minutes.

Makes a 9- or 10-inch round

2 tablespoons olive oil

1 cup yellow cornmeal

1 cup masa harina

1 cup all-purpose flour

¼ cup sugar

1½ tablespoons baking powder

Salt

¼ cup olive oil

3 eggs

About ¼ cup cold water

2 avocados, diced

Avocado-Corn Waffles

xxxxxx

Makes about 6 waffles

1 cup all-purpose flour

1 cup yellow cornmeal

$1/4$ cup sugar

1 tablespoon baking powder

Pinch of salt

$1/4$ cup olive oil

2 eggs

About $1/2$ cup buttermilk

1 avocado, diced

Served with butter only or with syrup, these are a delicious change of pace. Try them some Sunday morning.

Heat the waffle iron. Mix together the flour, cornmeal, sugar, baking powder, and salt. Beat the oil and eggs together, and add to the flour mixture. Add enough buttermilk to form a thick batter. Do not over-mix; a few lumps are all right. Gently fold in the avocado. Bake as per instructions for your waffle iron.

Avocado-Macadamia Nut Bread

xxxxxx

This bread is delicious as is—or try serving it with a scoop of sliced strawberries.

Makes 1 standard loaf

Preheat the oven to 350 degrees F. Prepare a baking pan by oiling and dusting with flour. Cream the butter and sugar together until fluffy. Beat in the eggs, avocado, and grated gingerroot and set aside. Sift together the flour, baking powder, cinnamon, and nutmeg. Add to the avocado mixture alternately with the water, folding in only until all dry ingredients are incorporated. Do not over-mix or the cake may be tough in texture. Gently fold in the macadamia nuts. Pour the batter into the prepared baking pan and put in the center of the oven for 45 minutes to an hour or until a slim skewer inserted into the center comes out clean. As soon as you remove the cake from the oven, pour the baker's syrup over it and allow the cake to sit in the pan until it has cooled a bit. Then remove it from the pan and allow to sit on a wire rack until completely cool.

1 stick softened (not melted) butter or margarine

1 cup sugar

2 eggs

1 large ripe avocado, mashed

1 teaspoon grated fresh gingerroot

2 cups all-purpose flour

1 tablespoon baking powder

1 teaspoon cinnamon

$1/2$ teaspoon nutmeg

$1/2$ cup cold water

1 cup chopped macadamia nuts

$1/2$ cup baker's syrup (recipe follows)

BAKER'S SYRUP

Put all ingredients in a saucepan and bring to a boil. Reduce heat to simmer for about 10 minutes. This may be used on many baked goods. On sweet breads, it gives a beautiful sheen, and it helps make cakes, quick breads, and muffins moist and tender. Any excess may be kept in a jar in the refrigerator for months. Heat it before using.

Makes about 2 cups

2 cups water

1 cup sugar

$1/4$ stick butter

2 tablespoons vanilla

Avocado-Apricot Bread

xxxxx

Makes 1 standard loaf

2 cups all-purpose flour

1 tablespoon baking powder

1/2 teaspoon salt

1 teaspoon nutmeg

1 stick butter

1 cup sugar

2 eggs

2 avocados, mashed

1 tablespoon vanilla extract

2/3 cup chopped dried apricots

2/3 cup chopped nuts

1/2 cup chopped candied ginger (optional)

About 1/4 cup water

Baker's syrup (see page 69)

On the ranch at Lake Ellsinore, in addition to raising poultry (our major commercial enterprise), we also grew walnuts, apricots, and almonds. We ate fresh apricots all during the season and dried them to use throughout the rest of the year. This recipe is a variation on one my mother developed to take advantage not only of our ongoing supply of avocados, but also our bounty of apricots and nuts. You may use almonds or walnuts or a combination thereof. If you are one of those who dislikes ginger, it's fine to leave it out.

Preheat the oven to 350 degrees F. Oil and flour a standard loaf pan.

Sift the flour, baking powder, salt, and nutmeg together. Set aside. Cream the butter and sugar together in a large bowl until fluffy, then beat in the eggs one at a time. Add the avocado and vanilla and blend well. Add the apricots, nuts, and ginger and incorporate thoroughly. Add the flour mixture, a bit at a time, stirring in after each addition. Add enough water to form a stiff batter. Pour into the prepared baking pan and place it in the center of the preheated oven. Bake for 45–60 minutes or until a slim skewer inserted into the center comes out clean. As soon as it comes out of the oven, paint liberally with baker's syrup.

Avocado–Cheddar Biscuits

xxxxxx

These unusual yet delicious biscuits can be a bit tedious to make. Do not expect the dough to handle the same way as regular biscuit dough. These make an excellent accompaniment to a light meal such as salad or soup.

Preheat the oven to 500 degrees F.

Sift the flour, baking powder, sugar, salt, and chili seasoning together into a bowl. Use a wire pastry blender to cut the butter into the flour mixture. Add the grated cheese and toss. Add water and, using a table fork, stir until all the ingredients are moistened. You want a dough that is not sticky yet still quite malleable. Turn the dough out onto a lightly floured surface and knead ever so gently. Over-working the dough will result in tough biscuits.

Pat the dough out to about ¼ inch thick. Cut into 1½-inch rounds. With the egg wash, paint the outer rim of half of the rounds. Place a piece of avocado in the center of the egg-painted rounds. Set a second round of dough on top of each. Pinch the edges to seal, and use your hands to reform them into nice round biscuit shapes. Place about 1 inch apart on a baking sheet lined with parchment. Place in the oven for 5 minutes, then reduce the heat to 350 degrees F and bake for another 20–25 minutes or until golden brown.

Makes about 1 dozen

2 cups all-purpose flour

1 tablespoon baking powder

$^1/_4$ cup sugar

Pinch of salt (optional)

2 teaspoons chili seasoning

1 stick cold butter, cut into very small pieces

$^1/_2$ cup grated extra-sharp Cheddar cheese

$^1/_2$–$^2/_3$ cup cold water

Egg wash (1 egg beaten with 1 tablespoon cold water)

1 avocado, cut into $^1/_2$-inch pieces

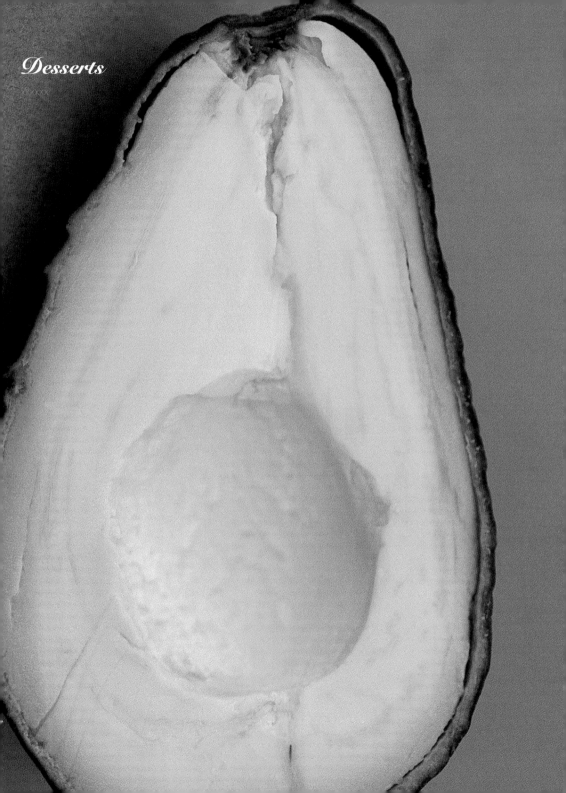

Desserts

Avocado Fool

xxxxxx

If you've never thought of avocados as a dessert, you have cut yourself off from a whole world of delectable endings. This recipe is a New World takeoff on the traditional English dish, "Fool," so called because it is so easy that even a fool can make it. In the English countryside it is made with seasonal soft fruits.

Mash the avocados exceedingly well and push through a sieve. Add the lime juice and stir. Whip the cream until it is very thick but not yet holding peaks. Slowly whip in the sugar, nutmeg, vanilla, and rum. Continue whipping until the cream holds soft peaks. Add several spoonfuls of whipped cream to the avocado and gently fold in to lighten. Then gently fold this avocado mixture into the remaining cream. Put into an attractive serving dish and chill thoroughly. Serve with a garnish of fresh lime slices and sprigs of fresh mint. This is a true summer refresher.

Variation Add about 1 cup of sliced strawberries to the fool before chilling. Garnish with whole strawberries and sprigs of fresh mint.

Serves 4–6

2 very ripe avocados

Juice of 1 lime

1 cup extra-heavy whipping cream

$1/2$ cup sugar, or to taste

$1/2$ teaspoon nutmeg

1 teaspoon vanilla extract

1 tablespoon dark rum

Avocado-Pear Dessert

xxxxxx

Serves 1

½ avocado, sliced

½ pear, sliced

1–2 tablespoons crumbled blue cheese

Port wine

Freshly ground black pepper

This dish is deliciously different and a wonderfully light dessert to serve after an elegant meal—and it's easy, too.

Arrange alternating slices of avocado and pears on a dessert plate. Sprinkle with crumbled blue cheese. Drizzle a bit of Port wine over all and top with a few grindings of pepper. You might even add a beautiful big strawberry with its stem still on.

Avocado-Strawberry Frappé

xxxxx

Serves 2

Your taste buds will spring to life with this frivolous frappé.

1 large ripe avocado, diced
1 cup sliced strawberries
1 cup crushed ice
1 cup whipping cream
$1/2$ cup sugar, or to taste
Juice of 1 lime
Whole strawberries,
for garnish
Fresh mint,
for garnish

Put all ingredients into the jar of your blender and pulse until well blended. Pour into elegant glasses and garnish with a whole strawberry and a sprig of fresh mint.

Avocado Cranberry Sherbet

xxxxx

Serves 3–4

Hass avocados and cranberry juice—two midwinter traditions—make this a perfect addition to your holiday table.

1 envelope
unflavored gelatin
1 cup cold water
1 cup cranberry juice
Juice of 1 lime
1 cup sugar, or to taste
2–3 ripe avocados,
mashed well

Sprinkle the gelatin on the water and allow to sit until it softens. Heat slowly until the gelatin dissolves. Add the cranberry juice, lime juice, and sugar, and bring to a boil. Remove from heat and allow to cool. Beat in the avocado. Follow directions for freezing Avocado Ice Cream (see page 78).

Avocado-Strawberry Chiffon Pie

xxxxxx

Don't miss the chance to share this springtime treat with friends and family.

Makes 1 8- to 9-inch pie

Sprinkle the gelatin on top of the water and allow to sit until it has softened. Beat the egg yolks, sugar, and milk together in a saucepan. Add the softened gelatin and stir over moderate heat until the sugar has completely dissolved. Continue to cook, whisking, for another 2–3 minutes. Remove from heat and whisk in the avocado and lime juice. Cool. Beat the egg whites until they hold peaks, and gently fold them into the avocado mixture. Fold in the strawberries and pour into the pie shell. Refrigerate until set. Garnish with whole strawberries and sprigs of fresh mint.

1 envelope unflavored gelatin

1/2 cup cold water

2 eggs, separated

1 cup sugar

1 1/2 cups milk

2 avocados, mashed

Juice of 2 limes

1 cup sliced strawberries

8- to 9-inch baked pie shell

Whole strawberries and sprigs of fresh mint, for garnish

Avocado Ice Cream

xxxxxx

Makes about
1½–2 quarts

4 cups (1 quart)
whipping or heavy cream

6–8 large avocados,
mashed (about 6 cups)

1½ cups sugar, or to taste

½ teaspoon nutmeg

1 tablespoon vanilla extract

You don't have to have an ice cream churn or ice cream maker to make ice cream. With a bit of care you can make it in a flat container in your freezer.

Mix all ingredients together well. If you have an ice cream churn or ice cream maker, follow the manufacturer's directions. If you do not have either, pour the mixture into flattish pans, such as standard loaf pans, that can go in the freezer. Place them in the freezer and check every half hour. As soon as any ice crystals form, stir them back into the mixture. Continue to do this until all the mixture has turned to ice cream. (It will take several hours.) Once it is the consistency of ice cream, you may put it in a storage container to keep. If you don't keep breaking up the ice crystals, the whole thing will turn to a solid lump of ice and be rather unremarkable.

INDEX